Books by Robert Hillyer

THE RELIC AND OTHER POEMS
1957

THE SUBURB BY THE SEA
1952

THE DEATH OF CAPTAIN NEMO
1950

POEMS FOR MUSIC: 1917–1947
1947

These are Borzoi Books,
published by Alfred A. Knopf in New York

The Relic & other poems

The Relic & other poems

ROBERT HILLYER

New York, Alfred A. Knopf
1957

Library of Congress catalog card no. 57–10308 © Robert S. Hillyer

This is a Borzoi Book, published by Alfred A. Knopf, Inc.

Acknowledgements

Acknowledgements are due to the editors of the following periodicals for permission to reprint poems that originally appeared in their pages:

Tomorrow for 'Intermezzo'

The Atlantic Monthly for 'One Kind of Colloquy' and 'In My Library, Late Afternoon'

The Freeman for 'The Bats'

The New Yorker for 'The Relic', 'Rough Winds Do Shake the Darling Buds of May', 'The Horsetail', 'The Cardinal Flower', 'The Marauders', 'Barcarolle', 'The Victim', 'The Scar', 'An Old-Fashioned Fourth', 'Overture', 'Fog', 'Light, Variable Winds', 'Proteus', 'The Ivory Tower', 'Under Yonder Beech Tree', 'The Eternal Return', 'The Suburb by the Sea', 'On the Narrow Brink of Dawn', 'After the Antiques Show', 'In the Shadowy Whatnot Corner'

The New York Herald Tribune for 'Departing Song Sparrows' and 'The Wild Philosopher'

The New York Times for 'Nocturne'

The New York Times Book Review for 'The Hammock in the Orchard' and 'A Bookman's Poem for Christmas'

The Indian P.E.N. Magazine for 'Time'

The Saturday Review of Literature for 'Academic Spring'

The Vineyard Gazette (Edgartown, Martha's Vineyard) for 'The Misses Adams'

'The Bats' was given the Borestone Mountain Poetry Award as the best poem of 1953 in American and English magazines, and was reprinted in the anthology *Borestone Mountain Poetry Awards*, 1953.

'In My Library, Late Afternoon' tied for first place in the Borestone Mountain Poetry Awards as the best poem of 1955 in American and English magazines, and was reprinted in the anthology *Borestone Mountain Poetry Awards*, 1955.

'Intermezzo' and 'In the Shadowy Whatnot Corner' were reprinted in the anthology *New Poems by American Poets*, edited by Rolfe Humphries and published by Ballantine in 1953.

'The Ruined Castle of Manorbier', under the title 'Manorbier', appeared originally in *The Dial* in 1928 and was reprinted in *The Collected Verse of Robert Hillyer*, published by Alfred A. Knopf in 1933 and awarded the Pulitzer Prize in 1934.

I also wish to make happy and grateful acknowledgment of my twenty-five years of association, marked by this present volume, with my publishers. To Alfred and Blanche Knopf, friends whom I have long held in admiration and affection, and to my many other friends in the offices of Alfred A. Knopf, I wish to extend my thanks for the best presentation of my work to the public which I could hope for.

ROBERT HILLYER

Contents

V Reminiscences

1 Familiar Acres

The Relic

A murmuring in empty shells
Recalls the ocean's undertone,
But not a wisp of music dwells
In this small skull of dulcet bone—
A thrush's skull, miraculous
Among dead leaves and threads of ice,
This delicate contrivance was
The sounding board of Paradise.

Beneath the tree lies music's skull,
The tree a skeleton of spring,
And both, perhaps, are beautiful
Though leaves and thrush no longer sing;
But, growing old, I have a reason
For wishing some divine delay
Could hold a song beyond its season
And hide the thrush's skull away.

The Cardinal Flower

Cold and amber
the shallow water,
shadowed by hemlocks;
there the cardinal
flower in August,
rooted in pebbles,
smolders dark red.
There, I remember,
we two swam,
and clambered on wet rocks,
part of primordial
earth in the awe-struck
hush of late summer.
There we are still,
no doubt, to the hearkening
shadow, our laughter
braided through brawling
waters audibly.
That is the country
I never escaped from.

The Victim

The hummingbird that darts and hovers
Made one fatal dart—alas!—
Against a counterfeit of flowers
Reflected in the window glass.
When four-o'clocks had sunk in shadow,
The window caught an extra glint
Of color, like the sudden rainbow
Arching the purple firmament.
Transcendent are the traceries
Illusion weaves to set a snare;
The quick competitor of bees,
Trusting his universe of air
For flight and honey, dazzled so
In quest of sweetness, was waylaid
By something hard that had a glow
Brighter than that the garden made.
Illusion shatters; the ideal
Is much more ruthless than the real.
The visionary hummingbird
Hit nothingness, and hit it hard.

The Singers

In unconsuming fire
    on leafing pyre,
the bird suspended there
    half earth, half air,
and wholly fire, fine-spun
    from south and sun,
the phoenix from his myth
    emerging with
my heart, articulate
    to be his mate:
after all winter long
    their dual song
of spring returning, spring
    returning. Sing,
O unconsumed yet burning,
    spring's returning!

Departing Song Sparrows

Farewell, song sparrows of spring,
Pausing once more to sing
Before your southward flight
Your crystal song,
Leaving us to the white
Dream winter-long
Of your returning.
Beneath the hazy flare
Of autumn, fields are bare
Except for milkweed fluff
Adrift on the hesitant air
And the smoke of leaves burning.
Farewell, our season yields
To time. There was song enough
Perhaps, for with changing mood
We look to the silent fields
And find them good.

The Horsetail

The spindly weed named horsetail (I can see
Small reason for the name) was once a tree
Aeons ago, so huge its upper boughs
Were lost in vapors from the reeking sloughs.
The pterodactyl, with a raucous scream,
Flapped to its jointed branches through the steam,
Witless of Nature's simple and succinct
"Reduce your stature or become extinct."
Alone amid that monstrous arboretum,
The philosophic horsetail (*Equisetum*)
Shrank through millenniums, until it stood
Twelve inches high amid another wood.

Surviving modestly, today it sees
The final humbling of ancestral trees,
Whose affluent decay from ancient soil
Is pumped by derricks ravenous for oil—
A million years of verdancy refined
To verdant millions of another kind.
The thin, ascetic plant, still running rife,
Deathless through trimming its demands on life,
Achieves its green, perennial intent;
While on vain errands or destruction bent,
My own coevals through the reeking sky
Like witless pterodactyls clatter by.

Bobwhite

Through hottest days the bobwhite sings;
His two-toned, reedy whistle rings
Windblown, familiar on this lawn,
Or to remoter green withdrawn,
At one with evening as with dawn.

His other name, the quail, suggests
Gunshot and slaughter-emptied nests;
The squinting eye, the flabby grin,
As the curst hunter closes in.

Bobwhite—I call him what he calls
Himself, though often he'll repeat
The first of his cool syllables
As though to quench the summer heat—
Small sun-defier, to whose golden
Note my summer is beholden.

The Marauders

Being death's foe, I can't make use
Of death to quell the rabbits; therefore,
They girdle saplings and reduce
To shreds the plantings I most care for.

They spurn the weeds, they shun the burrs,
And, as though versed in catalogues,
Choose but the best, these connoisseurs,
Scornful of men, alert to dogs.

At night my headlights pick them out
Bold in the field, of every size
From buck to baby. When I shout
They hop an inch in pained surprise.

With time, small things grow larger. Doom
Speaks from the dead rose on the lattice;
By night the dancing rabbits loom
Sub specie aeternitatis.

One Kind of Colloquy

Here in the garden, strolling slowly
With a young poet who is wholly
Rapt in his own imagination,
I leave to him the conversation,
Knowing that through his golden mist
I'd loom, a sad materialist.

How creature comforts come to be
A substitute for ecstasy!
Wordsworth, romantic though he was,
Confessed how revelations pass;
And Henry Vaughan, light's own true son,
Observed the same phenomenon.
Blake moved in radiance to the end
As Catherine saw his soul ascend
Clapping its hands; and Shakespeare, after
Storming the globe's extremest rafter,
Vanished in more tempestuous magic
Beyond the comic or the tragic.
But, on the whole, the poets mostly,
Becoming less remote and ghostly,
Repeat with stresses more intense
Our general experience,
When dithyrambic dreams attract
Less than the fantasies of fact.

But why should I anticipate
This younger poet's future state?
He speaks of love that moves the stars,
Of revolution ending wars,
Abstractions realer than the real,
And, clear as crystal, the Ideal.
His nostrils quiver in response
To ethers that I savored once;
His thoughts like angels climb the rungs
Of ladders toward the gift of tongues.
How accurately he can spell
The name of the Ineffable!

Not yet acknowledging the birth
Of beauty from component earth,
He floats through flowers that yesterday
Were treated with manure and spray,
And sees them vaguely as pale gems
Suspended without roots or stems.
All air and fire, his darting sense
Spurns the two coarser elements—
Water, from which we first were born,
And earth, to which we all return.
Nostalgic for such vision, ah
How can I say, *"J'ai vu tout ça"*?

Better for him to keep the rapture
That I have known but can't recapture;
Better for me my narrower joy
That views of distance would destroy.
Our difference breeds harmoniousness;
His talk attunes my silences.
On this bright lawn, this flowering slope,
Keats could have bared his soul to Pope,
And wit relived the age of hope.

The Mockingbird Awakes and Sings at Night

The mockingbird awakes and sings at night
More beautifully than the nightingale,
Whose poet-haunted song,
More by association than delight,
Enchanted me
In dark beech woods beside the Baltic Sea.

Now as the moonlight fades along
The firefly-crinkling air
And moves on toward the western hill,
The mockingbird, untouched by myth or rhyme
And never having heard the nightingale,
Still can repeat, instinctive plagiarist,
Note by note,
That laureate melody of night and time.

More often strange inventions tune his throat
To the world drifting in the lunar mist,
And never twice the same the unearthly scale
From which he plucks his themes—
Nocturnes as changeable as streams
That flow away forever yet remain,
Improvisations not to be heard again.

With such variety of song
And bantering interlude
He makes his own myth from the solitude,
Singing as long
As the moon hovers on the western hill.
At last, ascending on one fluttering trill,
He flies away to silence. Only then
Are we aware the faded moon has gone.

Fields in November

The moon on these withered fields,
The pale, transforming light,
Gives them a glimmer of green,
The ghost of a summer night.
Long, long ago, it seems now,
When men were young in this land
Where nobody ever dreams now,
Except for the moon, there was magic
Over the world, and the path
Was open to south and north,
Till the wrinkled angel of wrath
Forbade that a man go forth
To the sun or the moon as he chose,
To the garden where he arose,
Or the mountain of silent snows.
I, like the rest, have lost much
Of my sight, hearing, and touch;
And I look on the breathing fields
In the glow of the moon and wonder
Where it has gone, that magic
Which led to the path beyond,
Where a man could be merry in spring
Forever, or sleep like a king
On the mountain of frozen thunder.

Nocturne

Over the cold hill the half-sun burning
Dull in its embers, and one leaf turning
Slowly down air; the white winter nearing
Through black frozen hours, long hours before morning;
The dead dark coming, the cold heart yearning
For home, for that room safe walled from the warning
Of the death beyond dying, the fear beyond fearing—
But look! You are loved, you were missed from the room,
And someone with a lantern is coming through the clearing,
Someone with a lantern on the path toward home.

The Bats

These caverns yield
But vampires upside down.
Better the field or town
Than exploration such as this.
These creatures of antithesis
With webbed unfeathered wings
Will shrink away from our electric wink
Lest they be dazzled to the dark of things.

Through stalactites
Of lancets in reverse
Their muffled flights rehearse
A foray on the world of sleep.
These are our underdreams that keep
Our secrets from ourselves,
The lark become half rodent in that dark
Wherein the downward mountain climber delves.

Seal all, before
In ragged panic driven
These nightwings pour to heaven
And seal us from our natural sun.
Of two forbidden trees, there's one
Untampered with till now,
Where throng, with their inaudibly high song,
The bats headdown from roots that are its bough.

The Girl in the Garden

After the long dry season
I look from the eastern window
Conversant with the dawn.
I will not speak a word;
My finger on my lips
Enjoins the leaves to silence.
Delicate is the morning,
The threshold of hesitant autumn
With no hint of farewell.

Summer was curled to a parchment
By drought and withering heat
That were deadlier than a winter.
But suddenly into my garden
One evening in the starlight
Came the lady, the sister of flowers.
She merely touched them in passing,
And they lifted up as though starlight
Had fallen as slanting rain.

The dawn of hesitant autumn
Spun from the dew and the sunlight
Reveals the unfading garden
In the country where I have dreamed.
Music attends her waking,

The girl who walked in my garden.
As the sun lifts up her eyelids
She will come to the eastern window,
And the leaves may begin their song.

Intermezzo

By the lake the orchards lie
Half in shadow, half in sun.
We were mortal, you and I;
We were parted. Now, as one,
We leave the shadow for the sun.

When I died I walked away
Down a long suburban street
Where the feathery elms of May
Arched as in a forest aisle.
There I walked as evening fell
Knowing that we two would meet
When the sickle moon was curled
Round the windmill by the well.

And you whispered with a smile,
"If you waken, you will weep;
That was in another world;
Now lie down, lie down and sleep."

Princess, if the lakes were dry,
And the orchard paths were frozen,
Would you still, unchanged as I,
Choose the lover you have chosen?

II Salt Airs

Overture

This record played in the room has lost all the music
I heard that night far out at sea:
I was alone in my sailboat, the sail breathing
slackly the light airs, the ripple at the bow
a placid murmur, and the tall mast
a slim black needle plying the North Star—
no one within miles of me, except where to starboard
the lights of a tug signalled three barges in tow,
and beyond that, off the invisible shoreline,
the flashing white and red of the lighthouse—
this music came from my radio in the darkness
and told me that I must sail alone
until, in some harbor known to the composer
but which I could barely surmise,
I arrived at dawn and dropped anchor and rowed ashore
in another dream beyond the starlight of this one,
the friends I have never found crowding the wharf,
waiting with welcome. The music came to an end,
but the eternal ship moved on to a rhythm
deeper than the keel or the waters under the keel,
and higher than the North Star over the masthead riding.

Barcarolle

The long stems of the water lilies
tangle the paddle; the canoe
held among lotus and amaryllis
halts in the water garden. Few
are the birds in the trees that ring the pool;
only the hermit thrush still sings
in the unfathomed depth of cool
greenery fresh from hidden springs.
Few are the birds, and quite alone
is the man amid the summer maze,
adrift on this remote lagoon
as though eternity were his.
Perhaps it is; he may have passed
beyond the flickering of days.
Into a peace profound as this
the pebble of his heart was cast.

Fog

Tempests lift the sea, but their howling onrush
also nerves the strength in the hands of helmsmen
gauging slants of waves and the prow that climbs them,
    true to a hair's breadth.

Fog it is we fear, when familiar headlands,
wharf, and shoreside turf, and the village housetops
—smudged mirages—vanish, and vaulted ghostland
    closes around us.

Air and water mingle in seamless twilight.
Only near the hull there is liquid darkness
still discernible as a patch of ocean
    feathered with salt foam.

Cry of sea gull, clang of the lone bell buoy,
voices inarticulate blown from nowhere,
muffled chugs of engines from all sides haunt us,
    lost in the gray drift.

Chill pervades our bones, as though we were made of
fog ourselves; our hands are benumbed, our eyebrows
furred with wet, like eaves in the rain that blur the
    windows beneath them.

Solitude imagines a looming iceberg,
rocks ahead, or reefs, or a crazy speedboat,
or, in wisps of vapor along the fog bank,
    faces of drowned men.

Where is safe to head but forever eastward?
Then, not quite believing the hint of daylight,
first we feel a warmth and perceive a vague form
    sharpen to contours.

Fog and fear together dissolve in sunburst.
Number 4 red nun is abeam to starboard.
Ah, that landfalls could be the home-port always
    when we are fogbound!

Light, Variable Winds

This is the getting-nowhere breeze
That tries the soul of mariners—
The reason that the Seven Seas
Are peopled with philosophers.

We come about or jibe, to learn
That wind can box the compass, too,
Adroitly turning as we turn,
Adverse no matter what we do.

Still, better than dead calm, at least
It does impel us back and forth,
Giving the west some hope of east,
The south mirages of the north.

Hardened philosophers, we thrive
On facts we cannot overcome
As in vague twilight we arrive
Where in vague dawn we started from.

The Scar

For forty years and more my hand has shown
The scar where once a fishhook tore the flesh.
The body bears these grudges of its own.
The mind would let them go, but scars refresh
Unwilling memory. Owing to this mark,
One summer moment at Menemsha Bight
Stays with me like a date cut in the bark
Of some old tree, though not another sight
Remains from that day, nor would any thought,
Except for this indelible reminder.
Each seven years a bodily change is wrought,
Yet cells renew the scar. The heart is kinder
That wears its wounds invisibly until
All names are lost, lacking a cicatrice.
The hand recalls the embedded fishhook still,
When love and memory long have been at peace.

The Misses Adams

In Chilmark—or West Tisbury,
Between an orchard and a bay,
The Misses Adams carded wool
Out on the lawn beneath a tree.
These midget sisters sang away
The finespun summer afternoon—
A quavering music out of tune,
But to a child's ear beautiful.

Their dignity stood four feet tall
In frocks of figured calico.
Behind them stood their house, a vast
Ancestral home for two so small,
Where dwelt a century ago
Great whaling captains and their wives,
Whose shadows lengthened as their lives
Grew legendary with the past.

The miniature sisters sang
Of how these giant folk sailed out
In barkentines across the sea
From Patagonia to Penang.
They sing their ballad still, no doubt;
But I can't find them now, because
I have forgotten which it was—
Chilmark or West Tisbury.

31

Time

Suddenly it is upon you. Your tall sloop
Takes care of you as you took care of her,
And conscience says, "Whatever have I done?"

This is no time to let self-pity stir;
Your glands mean nothing to Aldebaran,
Nor can old dogs set sail for Guadeloupe.

Time passes. Time is past. And yet to sit
With sick eyes gazing at the unanswering world
Would be to invoke all that you have abhorred.

Leave something to fair Nature, amply stored
With morning glories' heavenly blue unfurled—

Leave something to good luck and to the Lord,
Knowing that, after all, they have the wit.

III Borderlands

The Ivory Tower

Who knows through what mysterious tensions these
Strange pinnacles of personality
Are held in place? The crazy structure sprawls
Over a territory not prepared
For architecture. Here a turret sags
Into the sand; there, on a rock, one tower
Stands up beyond its place in the design,
And gargoyles counterbalance random shifts
From equipoise, or flying buttresses,
As late as yesterday, were improvised
Hastily over space to clutch a wall.

Some years ago this efflorescent structure
Could have been simplified, even rebuilt,
According to a modern analyst,
With low walls all of glass to gulp the sun,
And the interior plain as everyday.
But now it is too late—one column shifted,
One bit of tracery removed, yes, even
One tendril of this ivy vine clipped off,
And the whole delicately balanced thing
Would crash around our ears. It is fantastic,
But best left as it is. And, by the way,
I note it has outlasted all the bombings.

The Suspended Moment

What do those stolid trees whose umber shoulders
Rise beyond corn shocks listen for, as though
They would step forward from among the boulders
Their roots have split, and move without a sound
At some expected signal from the sky?
The sun has set, and all behind them lie
The piled-up embers of the afterglow,
And sudden chill arises from the ground.

Who is that standing shadowed by the trees,
Almost invisible where field meets glade?
This evening trembles with expectancies;
Amid lifelong, unreasonable contrition
I am afraid of time and of time's ending,
As though the luminous evening now descending
Were the world's last. I am afraid, afraid
Of the dark plunge to endless repetition.

That was the child's dream, the black, cliff-like mirrors
Repeating and repeating death and birth
Till, paralyzed with individual terrors,
He cried out for forgetfulness once more
And woke in the assuaging arms of night
As I do now; all outlines put to flight,
Except my hands, dim moths of air and earth,
Praying the prayer I dared not pray before.

The Heavenly Assurance

It is not easy when the years of rapture
Are over, and the nerves report the scene
In facts without illusions, to recapture
The early light in gardens briefly green
Smelling of summer in the bud, the sense
Hovering like a hummingbird between
The honeyed foretaste and experience—
It is not easy to recapture that,
So fresh, miraculous, so delicate.

But now and then unheralded there is
A rift among considered thoughts, a break
In daily logic, a quick surge of bliss
Such as George Herbert, Henry Vaughan, and Blake
With instantaneous dexterity
Caught before cynic Reason could awake
To chase the angels from the dooryard tree.
It passes, but amid our dull endurance
Leaves a bright hint, a heavenly assurance.

Scenic Railway

Strapped in our seats on time's great roller-coaster,
We are pulled slowly up through autumn haze,
Through winter chill, until late February,
When, with a brightening view of warmer days
We pause an instant on the breathless summit,
Then downward in accelerating glide
Through spring and the green-tunnelled summer plummet,
The sea on one side, flowers the other side—
Crocus to morning glory to the amber
Chrysanthemum frost-silvered in November.
Then under darkening skies we start the climb
All over, dreading the foreshortened hours
Of sunlight shrinking to pinpoints of time
And the frost silvering us like autumn flowers.
So have I ridden sixty turns and more—
My ancestors apparently lived well
To leave so many tickets at the door.
How many still are left? I will not dwell
On that or on the exit into dark
When, all my rides being over, I confront
The man who runs the whole amusement park,
And hear the inevitable "Do you want
Another batch of tickets, Mister?" What
Shall I reply to that? Do I—or not?

Three Guesses

Between the autumn trees three little girls
Saw three men passing, far away and hazy.
"Druids!" said Edith, shaking out her curls;
"Fishermen!" Violet said. "You are both crazy,"
Said Jane, "the Druids all died long ago,
And there's no stream. Those men are tramps, too lazy
To work and yet too nervous to stay still."

The three men parted halfway up the hill,
And one sought out a grove, remote and dim,
And with his Druid knife cut mistletoe.
One reached a river where he fished till dark.
The third one, setting all the dogs to bark,
Tramped on until the starlight cradled him.

Edith lay long awake that night and pondered.
Violet dreamed of rivers far away.
Jane, weaving endless computations, wondered
How much she could save up by New Year's Day.

The Magicians

We spin our illusions out from season to season
As the spider his shimmering web among four stems,
Or like the rainbow flung above roofed-in reason
From nowhere to nowhere, the roadway of water and gems.
Tell us a name—Semiramis, Tut-ankh-Amen,
Then it will flower like a Hindu conjurer's tricks;
With us it is the miraculous that is common,
From the course of the morning star to the banks of the Styx.
Here are the parallel lines converging in glory,
The song of the sirens, the pace of perpetual motion,
All things eternal, fixed, yet transitory
As the river of Heraclitus, the tides of the ocean.
Leave us at will if you are uneasy with splendor;
The dust in the sunbeam is winking the last of the day.
When the king comes it is time to dismiss the pretender—
But who could be harder to tell apart than they?

The Lost Music

In the underworld, O Orpheus,
How strangely sounded string and voice
Before the midnight throne of Dis.
In gardens of Persephone
Where ghosts of flowers that bloomed above
Blossom again all winter long,
How strangely living was your song!
The Queen embraced Eurydice,
Homesick for summer and for love,
And both stood unbelieving there
To hear your music from afar.

O Orpheus, on your return
How strangely sounded voice and string
Along the beams of living spring.
Those were your lyre when you were young;
But birds and beasts now shunned the sound
That once had charmed them, for the tone
Held echoes from a world unknown.
Eurydice, still lost among
The wandering shadows underground,
Heard nothing now; and daylight spurned
Dead music from the past returned.

The Eternal Return

Along how many Main Streets have I walked,
Greeting my friends, commenting on the weather,
Carrying bundles, wondering as I talked
If the brown paper bags would hold together.

At Christmas time with white breath blowing thin,
In spring when garden tidings are exchanged,
In autumn with the darkness closing in
And all the winter's work to be arranged.

Wherever I have lived—and many places
Have briefly seemed my permanent abode—
The shops on Main Street and the passing faces,
Beyond all history and change of mode,

Remain the same. And if while on a walk
I should encounter people who belong
In Main Streets of my past, I'd stop to talk
Without suspecting anything was wrong.

Even if I met someone who was dead,
I would discount the fact as in a dream.
Here things that lie behind are still ahead,
And calendars less final than they seem.

External accidents of time and space
Become, on Main Street, but illusory errors,
As all my incarnations, face to face,
Repeat themselves like people in two mirrors.

I greet acquaintances unchanged as I,
Stop for a moment, comment on the weather,
And at the corner, as I say goodbye,
Pray God my paper bundles hold together.

Flight from the Island

Everything on the island failed that year;
The flowers in early June climbed over each other
Blooming hysterically for a week or two,
Then all were suddenly gone and the gardens bare.
Not so much as a bud for the grave of my brother
Was to be found. By July the season was through.

Then the great drought set in. The sea itself
Seemed to recede from the island toward the horizon
As though the tides were afraid of becoming tainted.
The seagull-deserted beach was a glaring shelf
With shells looking like skulls of steers and bison
On a western desert as we have seen it painted.

No summer visitors came that year, and under
The wharf sheds all their fancy boats dried up
As spreading seams let fall the flakes of calking.
The islanders, deprived of crops and plunder,
Took to their boats and fished for flounder and scup,
While by the fences their wives did little talking.

One old man said Bikini was the cause,
That all the islands have their roots together,
And when one dies the others seem to wilt.

This was rejected, after a thoughtful pause,
But all agreed the bomb had ruined the weather
As common sense could prove right up to the hilt.

Then in late August came the mysterious quaking
That shook the island from the depths of ocean
Or twitched it gently like a throbbing nerve.
It felt as though a thunderous surf were breaking
Far off and sending vibratory motion
From somewhere out beyond the planet's curve.

I was among the men who left that autumn,
Thinking the mainland safer than the island
Where things might well go worse from year to year.
But even here, up from the deep sea bottom
The tremors start and quiver to the highland—
And how shall we escape them anywhere?

IV Observations

Proteus

I have no enemies today;
I may have had them yesterday,
Tomorrow I shall have some, maybe.
Not two days running has the same
Identity assumed my name
Since I was an unchristened baby.

The wicked godmother who brings
Envenomed gifts to christenings
Went mumbling down ancestral hallways,
Decreeing I should never be
A self-continued entity
But doomed to metamorphose always.

The things my name has done and said,
Like stories in a book I've read,
I scan with comments quite objective.
I am, perforce, indifferent
To future deeds I can't prevent
With their appropriate corrective.

Today alone is my concern.
Tomorrow—why, I well may burn
For sins that were my someone-else's;
Or if good fortune in his place
Should substitute a man of grace,
Rise, singing *gloria in excelsis*.

49

Cock of the Wind

His will as the weather's,
The weathercock glances
Bright in the sun
On his pinnacle perch.
Enamelled in feathers,
He whirls to his fancies:
He is the one
Whom they worship in church—

He can see them below—
And he also is certain
His whirling determines
The way the winds veer,
And when winds do not blow
And he perches inert on
His spindle, his sermons
Have spellbound the air.

So effect becomes cause
In his doting complacence,
As high on the steeple
He twirls in self-love.
All sound is applause,
All hush is obeisance—
Below, merely people,
And no god above.

A Popular English Novel

When I was a boy I lived on a large estate
With acres of gardens and ornamental waters;
Dragons surmounted the Jacobean gate,
And I was called "Master Nigel" by the gardener's daughters.
Everyone knew his place, from the comic peasant
To the marquis with his preserve of deer and pheasant.

A Henry James contrivance of protocol
Is the scene I spread before you of English fashion—
Garden parties to soothe the patrician soul
And tennis matches to soothe fastidious passion.
Then came the War—and, by the way, I had
Grown up by then, though at heart I remained a lad.

The War came, and if I do say so who shouldn't,
In view of my sheltered background, I did well;
My noncoms risked their lives when, too imprudent,
I led them through barrages of shot and shell.
Meanwhile in London, my wife—perhaps I neglected
To say I had one—my wife did the unexpected.

It wasn't wholly her fault. Wars tend to level
Distinctions between the classes, do what you can.
In uniform, the footman, a handsome devil,

Would pass, except for his speech, for a gentleman.
I was willing, of course, to forgive my wife, but she—
She left the house and spoke of forgiving me!

In the nineteen chapters that follow, you find an extensive
And spiritual message in elevated style.
My hair just touched with gray, I am handsome, pensive,
And won my second wife with a whimsical smile.
That marriage itself denotes my emancipation,
Because, to be frank, she isn't quite of my station.

A Popular American Novel

Creatures in this modern novel
Slink from cabin into hovel,
Dragging with their weary selves
Druggëd girls and draggled elves.
Give me pick and give me shovel,
Let oblivion's lower shelves
Deep in shale where no one delves
Bury them; below the levels
Known to mice or men or devils
Where the vampire weakly wails
When his heart is plugged with nails,
In unconsecrated gravel
Where no critics praise or cavil,
Where no royalty avails
From publicity or sales,
Take the psychopathic drivel,
Dying whine, infected snivel—
Though it won a brief approval
It is time for its removal.
Give me pick and give me shovel
To inter the modern novel.
Thanks . . .

        What's that? Do you insist?
Good! Throw in the novelist.

Rough Winds Do Shake the Darling Buds of May

Wool, you need wool in this weather,
  Whatever the calendar says;
Take from the whole year together
  The most deceptive of days,
  And two thirds of them will be May's.

Summer, the summer is coming—
  But summer has not yet come;
Noontide is vibrant with humming
  Of insects that soon will be dumb
  While the telegraph wires will hum.

Undeterred by the nagging northwester,
  Golden the dandelion glows;
Sorrel and *planta genesta*
  Bloom while the mad wind blows,
  But never a lily or rose.

Tent caterpillars gnaw the wild cherry;
  The Japanese beetles hatch out;
Cold germs are belligerent—very,
  And if you go wandering about
  Without wool, they will seize you, no doubt.

Wool, it is wool you should wear now,
    Though reading these lines you will say,
"What a joke for this piece to appear now,
    On this marvelous morning of May!"
    Ah well—then have it your way.

The Wild Philosopher

The wild philosopher surveyed the scenes
Where rubble of humanity's best thought
Lay in the after-fumes of gaunt machines,
Decided the whole case was hopeless, sought
Comfort in his wine cellar, that cool cave,
And taking sundry bottles from the shelf,
Quoted Li Po: "Seeing all men behave
Like drunkards, why stay sober by myself?"
As he refilled his glass from time to time
Snatches of music, memories of youth
Came back to him, and suddenly sublime
With purpose as a man half crazed by truth,
He sprang up brandishing a new idea—
Nay, more than that, the whole world's panacea!

Under Yonder Beech Tree

The weeping beech tree forms a leafy cave
Cool as the hollow in a breaking wave;
There in a hammock made of woven mesh,
Mrs. Moran lays down her weary flesh.
The summer murmur, resonant and deep,
Vies with the shadows in persuading sleep.
Her pretty hands, her face as delicate
As shell, her feet too dainty for her weight,
All, frail as Dresden, seem not quite designed
With Mrs. M's anatomy in mind.
While appetite quells vanity, she dreams
Not of a lover but of chocolate creams.

One word might yet arouse her sense of duty
To trim the expanding pedestal of beauty,
But let it go unsaid. On sun-drenched days
The ghost of Gauguin or Gaston Lachaise
Might find in such heaped indolence of mood
A masterpiece of tropic amplitude.
Beauty is in the eye of the beholder:
Though she accumulates below the shoulder,
Mrs. Moran, asway in massive calm,
Suggests Tahiti and the coco-palm—
Full summer ease in one exotic touch
Amid a world that diets overmuch.

On the Narrow Brink of Dawn

Ah, could the lines composed at midnight hold
By day the glister that we thought was gold,
The letters eloquent at 2 a.m.
Retain the magic that dictated them!
Those phrases shaped in the inspiring hush
Are wit by lamplight and by daylight gush—
As friendships, after one effusive meeting,
Sink to acquaintanceships on second greeting.
The ardent overtures, the frank confessions
Seem the next morning to be indiscretions,
And many a scribbler by the midnight lamp
Had kept his standing had he lost his stamp.

Thoughts glide along their indolent canal
Between enticing growths of *fleurs du mal*,
And sentiment, with easy tears endued,
Renews old friendships best left unrenewed.
On current issues, lonely indignation
Writes to the newspapers for publication;
On love, the pen grown eloquent with hope
Scrawls postscripts even on the envelope;
On courage, "Sir, one well-considered line
Conveys my feelings toward you: I resign."
O stamps, be lacking! Mood, be transitory!
The telephone? But that's another story.

An Acquisition

In Muse's Bookshop, at the very back,
I purchased for ten cents a book of verse
To save the poet and that "Cousin Jack"
Whom he regarded warmly in a terse
Inscription on the flyleaf, from disdain;
Only to find that Cousin Jack had shed
Three other volumes by the family bard,
Each in its paper cover still unread,
And each presented with "my warm regard,"
Presented, dated, signed—all quite in vain.

I put down three more dimes and bought the lot:
This poet, long ago, had been my friend
As far as he was able, which was not
Much farther than the gaining of an end—
But memory has no need to judge the dead.
Going back ten years, I can see him sicken;
Going back twenty, proud and climbing high;
Going back thirty, pitifully stricken
With first experience of love's perfidy.
And, for that life, there's no more to be said.

And Cousin Jack? He must have been a savage
To sell these to a second-hand bookstore,
Where vulgar eyes of philistines could ravage

The metaphysics and the metaphor
That clutched at fame but chased the vogue too hard.
Yet maybe Cousin Jack is dead himself,
And all his books are in the bargain basement.
Well, there's an end. I'll put these on the shelf
Where, if I clip the ivy from the casement,
The sun will penetrate with warm regard.

After the Antiques Show

Wherever wealth takes up its brief abode
Antiques come rolling down the open road;
Truckloads of furniture in endless lines
Follow the signposts toward the dollar signs.
The handicrafts that fashioned them forgotten,
The roofs that sheltered them caved in and rotten;
These humble chattels of our forebears stood
In Newport once, and then in Hollywood,
And now, where tax-free oil provides a palace,
They make their weary pilgrimage to Dallas.

Spindle and spokes at rest, the spinning wheel
Stands idle next to its companion reel,
Still able to prepare the homespun wool
But fated to be quaint and beautiful.
The prices paid for lustre would have bought
The whole establishment where it was wrought.
A cradle rocks the kindling wood to sleep,
The banjo clock has no more time to keep,
And unancestral portraits look askance
On those who bought, yet claim, inheritance.

Soon will the wealth move on, we know not where,
But this we know—the antiques will be there,

Proving that those who chase the future cast
Acquisitive back glances toward the past,
Where, in the objects of a simpler age,
Fancy, at least, can find a heritage.
So dowagers evoke the sixteen-eighties
With someone else's *lares et penates*,
Who, now grown skeptical of hearth and home,
Whisper all night of travels yet to come.

The Suburb by the Sea

Here, in the suburb by the sea, the surf
Foams on the rocks that guard the private turf,
And in flood tides of autumn does not halt
But pours across and sows the lawns with salt,
To break against the walls of terraces
Where Roman gardens and Shakespearean trees
Embower the mansion and the formal hedge
From all directions but the water's edge.
How beneficial are the rich, whose pride
Pays for this ornamental countryside,
A park that otherwise had vanished hence
Or been maintained at government expense.

The pocket harbor floats the local tanker
And is so flecked with gleaming yachts at anchor
That, from afar, observers might suppose a
Tree had shed white leaves on Vallombrosa,
Until the yachts, to change the simile,
Spread wings like waterfowl and fly to sea.
Like birds, they migrate when the cold winds blow
And early winter dusts the air with snow.
The ice puts out, beneath the frosted moon,
A tentative webbed foot on the lagoon,
And mothers, to place débutantes on view,
Sublease a duplex on Park Avenue.

The suburb, ringed by housing projects, levelled
By taxes, and by satirists bedevilled,
Defaced by trade's encroaching sabotage,
Will shortly seem a lingering mirage.
With eyes that cherish what must soon expire,
I see it drift toward Nineveh and Tyre,
Its "Private Property—No Thoroughfare"
Shaken by city traffic roaring near.
No funds will serve, no sentiment avail,
To curb the influx from beyond the pale.
But after us the deluge! I shall be,
By then, in suburbs by a darker sea.

Espalier

How willful is that vine I worked to train
Against the lichened wall to bear me fruit,
Long pampered by alternate sun and rain
And the dark labor of the groping root;
Fair to some eyes, but never fair to mine;
So different from my ordered plan, the tangles
And wayward tendrils of this truant vine
Are idle as the shadow that it dangles.
This summer dance I will not witness longer,
Knowing my anger will give way to grief
When the skies darken, and the wind, grown stronger,
Plucks off the sumptuous folly, leaf by leaf—
Until, too much my likeness, is displayed
What pride could not control nor love persuade.

v Reminiscences

In My Library, Late Afternoon

In the dim library, my younger self
Drifts with possessive hands from shelf to shelf,
Haunting familiar volumes, he can quote them
More eloquently than the men who wrote them,
Because he adds a private overtone
From old associations of his own.
A four-line epigram by Francis Quarles
Glows with the winter sunset on the Charles,
Pale rain in Pomfret shimmers through Jane Austen,
Through Trollope blows the salt east wind of Boston,
And Gibbon's wit was sharpened all too well
As Europe at Versailles declined and fell.

The notion that old books can be bewitched
By aspects of a life they have enriched
Might strike the casual reader who pursues
Detective fiction down a maze of clues
As somewhat morbid—yet I find it more so
To read all night about a missing torso.
And the new critic, happy jargoneer,
Who makes obscure what once was fairly clear,
While literature, beneath his magic passes,
Replaces mirrors with distorting glasses,
Would sigh, consult his glossary, and then
Return to nineteen twenty-two again.

Ah, but some books, like those where flowers were pressed,
Indeed become a fragrant palimpsest.
Sir Thomas Browne, skilled Merlin of the mood,
My rapt and adolescent solitude
Evokes, with beauty made more beautiful
By blossoming from eyeholes of a skull.
Sonnets of Shakespeare, Sidney, and Rossetti,
Drayton's *Idea* and Spenser's *Amoretti*
Discourse of double loves, their own and mine,
With reminiscences in every line;
And manuscripts, both harbingers and mourners
Of too much joy, grow dusty in dim corners.

Gray-fingered druid shadows gather now
The mistletoe upon the Golden Bough;
King Arthur's barge and the Nicean bark
Rush with the wandering ocean toward the dark;
The awkward Don avoids one final fall
By leading Rosinante to her stall.
Unswayed by critics and by vogue undaunted,
I am content among the books I've haunted:
The oftener they're read, the more they give.
In them my cumulative past shall live
Until, our long collaboration done,
I melt in earth, they in the lexicon.

Academic Spring

Now learning is entangled with the weather,
And ever green shall be these studied pages
Where facts and youth and south wind blend together,
Impelling the live sap up trellised ages
To flaunt new leaves on vines of classic thought,
Refreshing the sere crowns on brows of sages,
While all the urgent push of spring is fraught
With birdsong from the groves beyond the dawn—
Those magic flutenotes never to be caught.
Under the great trees on the campus lawn
The girls in colors like embodied joys
Cluster and flutter, seemingly withdrawn
From seemingly indifferent groups of boys.

"Another year gone by," say the professors,
Putting aside the last examination;
They feel like portraits of their predecessors,
A little dark with time, for graduation
Holds reminiscence more than promise, more
Than learning's periodic consummation.
To those who watched their classes march to war
The hushed alumni of mortality
In cap and gown still haunt the Gothic door.

But now, by "Pomp and Circumstance" set free,
Seniors in blowing robes file slowly by,
While the south wind rides on from tree to tree,
And the white sun stands cloudless in the sky.

In the Shadowy Whatnot Corner

Blest be the bric-a-brac that still survives
Demolished houses and forgotten lives,
And, with a Dresden signal from the shelves,
Calls back the children who were once ourselves.
The French clock swings the mercury of time
Captive in glass and regular as rhyme.
The candelabra in their crystal lustres
Splinter a beam of light in rainbow clusters.
Swans die in their own music, roses in
Their own perfume, but roses from Pekin
And swans from Sèvres, having no scent or song,
Stay, while a hundred summers glide along.

Lovers from Meissen, clowns from Copenhagen,
Amorous cupids, innocently pagan,
Beribboned shepherds with their shepherdesses
Poised in forever unachieved caresses:
These beings, like ourselves, were shaped from clay,
But in such heat as burned their lusts away.
Frozen in flame, they glazed to chilly fire,
Immune from death and death's pale twin, desire,
Unless, on some dyspeptic morning, Sadie's
Wild duster tangles in the porcelain ladies,
Or Mrs. Fulsome, clumsy connoisseur,
As usual breaks what most appeals to her.

Tiffany glass, they tell me with a smile—
In fact, all *art nouveau*—is back in style.
The eighteen-forties, too, come in for praise,
Late Empire, and my opalescent vase,
Which makes me wonder where such things would be
If Style had swept the previous century.
The architect, to serve the vogue, uptilts
Greenhouses thirty stories high on stilts,
Supplanting walls of stone with sheets of glass.
Like "General Grant" and mansard these will pass,
While, cherished and unchanging, will remain
The only world that lasts—of porcelain.

The Hammock in the Orchard

Once more the hazy southwest wind prevails,
Blowing a vague mist over sea and sails,
And in old orchards indolently heaves
The unmown grass and filigree of leaves.
Deep summer drones a reminiscent tune
Through the long, languorous, hot afternoon,
Unveiling vistas of the past that seem
So real, reality becomes a dream.
It would not much surprise me to observe
An open trolley car lurch round the curve,
Or hear down quiet sidestreets the clip-clop
Of horses stumbling to a patient stop,
Or watch four-masted schooners Bangor bound
And proud sidewheelers churning up the Sound.
It would not much surprise me if I saw—
As I can almost see—my aunt-in-law,
Recumbent in the hammock slung between
These orchard trees that still are hale and green,
Her mouth agape in unbecoming slumber
Over some novel or Midsummer Number.

A rusty hook protruding from the bark
Of this old apple tree preserves the mark
Of summers long ago—my own first twenty—
When Kirk Monroe, the Rover Boys, and Henty

Gave way to Dickens, then a somewhat tardy
And frowned-upon enthusiasm for Hardy.
I captured the fringed hammock, though, but seldom:
My aunt-in-law, a most voluminous beldam,
Invited for the weekend, would make tracks
As soon as lunch was over, to relax
Beneath the fretted shade with summer reading
Designed as an escape from sports or weeding.
While tennis players practiced the new Lawford,
George Barr McCutcheon and F. Marion Crawford
In Graustark or in Rome beguiled Aunt Jane
Until the thunderheads dissolved in rain.
Anthony Hope she worshipped, and was fond
Of William Locke's *Beloved Vagabond*.
Ah, and what stammered words and flaming cheeks
Betrayed her, caught red-handed with *Three Weeks*!

Except in Hardy and in Madam Glyn,
Vice was unknown to fiction's heroine.
While seldom tempted, never taking chances,
The lovely girl was trapped by circumstances
In which the villain was empowered to try
The extra squeeze of hand, the glint of eye.
The hero, literally a holy terror,
Soon thrashed him to acknowledgment of error,
Whereat he vanished, or, contritely shedding

His sins, turned up as best man at the wedding.
Poor folk were worthy and the rich were kind;
Humor was lame but lambently refined;
And sometimes literature became more ample
In depth of moral purpose; for example,
Problems for readers not too easily bored
Were raised and solved by Mrs. Humphry Ward.

Explore your attics and your mustier shelves
To summon back the era for yourselves.
Then while the shrill northeaster, blind with rain,
Drowns all the world beyond the windowpane,
Your ghosts will come indoors and reassemble
To read beside the fire. You needn't tremble—
They'll be too lost in *Allan Quartermain*
Or *Hugh Wynne, Quaker* or the last Hall Caine
To note your presence, though perplexed a little
To find the leaves so mildewed and so brittle.
Only the shadow children, at the chime
Of the unfailing "once upon a time,"
Find wonderland behind the looking glass
And hear the winds among the willows pass
Over the jungle folk, the treasure islands,
Pale Camelot and Scotland's haunted highlands,
Just as they always were, for Time swings free
Before the whispered "Open sesame."

The First World War unleashed another age:
With *What Price Glory?* swear-words reached the stage;
With Michael Arlen and F. Scott Fitzgerald
The heroines set out to be imperilled.
Convention reeled before each brash newcomer,
And summer reading grew too hot for summer.
The hammock, weathered to a streaky gray,
Swung empty, and at last was tucked away
With *Little Colonel* books, *Monsieur Beaucaire*,
And Baedekers to towns no longer there.

Yet in the orchard where the grass grows high
And green leaves intercept the shining sky,
Dorothy Vernon steps from Haddon Hall,
Young Carthaginians breach the Roman wall,
Princes and paupers, sorcerers and thieves,
People the background tapestry of leaves,
And Life's long fiction, now so nearly done,
Is flicked back by the wind to Chapter One.

An Old-Fashioned Fourth

The glorious Fourth is tamed and has become
A holiday of regulated joys,
With speeches, songs, and dank officialdom,
While fireworks are proscribed as lethal toys
And nowhere seen but in the public parks
For the remote applause of girls and boys
Removed from jeopardy of flying sparks—
Spectators who are suitably astonished
When rockets bloom from coruscating arcs.
Firecrackers and brass cannon have been banished;
Torpedoes, packed in little bags of sand,
Have, with the horses they once frightened, vanished;
In fact, a pale decorum shrouds the land.

Once it was shrouded in gunpowder smoke
And hollow booms as giant crackers burst,
Breaking the hush as soon as daylight broke,
Continuing till nightfall, when the first
Rocket soared upward, trailing a thin blaze,
Followed by hundreds that in turn dispersed
Their Queen Anne's lace of jewel-tipped bouquets
Spearing the clouds. Meanwhile, our nether world
Glowed with the flares in green-and-scarlet haze,
And Chinese lanterns glimmered, pinwheels swirled
Their hissing firedance on the sidewalk tree—

And ah! the set piece of our flag unfurled
With forty-six stars in its galaxy!

The day dragged slowly, but at last it ended
As boys returned like battle-smudged dragoons;
A little breeze arose, the dew descended,
Then, lovelier than all, beneath the moon's
Disdainful chill, alive with warmth and light,
Floated the argosies of fire balloons
Along the driftways of the upper night.
Weaving through warps of noise their silent woofs,
They gradually cooled and sank from sight
To kindle haymows or dry shingle roofs,
Startling the darkness with tumultuous pyres
While horse-drawn engines, loud with clashing hoofs
And clanging gongs, plunged toward the scattered fires.

For days thereafter street and lawn were littered
With wagonloads of colorful debris;
Children were bandaged, parents were embittered,
Charred patches were revealed on grass and tree.
But, doubtless, every young incendiary
Would most enthusiastically agree
That even Christmases were secondary
To these wild holocausts that thrilled us yearly.
Concerning this, opinions well may vary;

I will but say I loved the old Fourth dearly
That threatened my survival each July;
But now it fades, and I remember merely
One bright balloon adrift in evening sky.

A Bookman's Poem for Christmas

Christmas is like two mirrors face to face
Within whose opposite reflections gleam
Bright Christmas trees repeating back through space
To where reality dissolves in dream.
For this one day is time wrenched out of place:
All Christmases that we remember seem
Part of this present joy and hurly-burly
That kept us late from sleep and woke us early.

Beneath the tree the packages are piled
That took so long to wrap and to adorn;
The glittering ribbon in a world gone wild
Is snapped, the sheets of gorgeous paper torn
With equal zest by grown-up and by child.
Then someone sounds a flourish on a horn
As grandmother and John, amid the din,
Arrive and, shaking off the snow, come in.

The shrillest groups and most redundant chatter
Surround the gifts that bulge, make noise, or shine,
The doll house and the dolls, toy trains that clatter,
Gear for one member of a baseball nine,
Contraptions that would baffle the Mad Hatter,
And television (through no fault of mine),
While till the end, because most easily guessed,
Are left the books, that shall outlast the rest.

The all-pervading scent of evergreen,
This most deciduous of holidays,
Invokes the past, as, looking in between
The tinselled boughs with reminiscent gaze,
I glance at the old books, and set the scene
With other gifts and givers, other ways,
When these same volumes, evergreen themselves,
Were bright newcomers to the study shelves.

Full fifty years the Wallypug's made merry
(My favorite hero—also G. B. Stern's).
The Peterkins and Captain January,
And others from the days of potted ferns
And Welsbach burners, though the vogue may vary,
Still claim young readers, while an old one turns
To greet the ghosts who in those vanished ages
In clear Spencerian inscribed the pages.

Where are the books the children now pass over,
Those many former favorites rejected?
We do not miss the boys whose name was Rover,
But (surely some day this will be corrected)
Where are those fairy tales with colored cover,
The Green, the Gold—the ones that Lang collected?
And poor Black Beauty! Till the horse come back,
Black Beauty but suggests a Cadillac.

Watching the children, well I understand
How magic may assume a different name:
Space is their Avalon, their Fairyland—
The more things change the more they are the same.
Their books have humor, too. No works are planned
With more astute perception of their aim,
Verse, fantasy, adventure tales aplenty,
And history—although no G. A. Henty.

Their elders find non-fiction still ascendant,
With books on art and travel, various Lives,
The Civil War (with fiction, too, attendant),
The sea and all that on its margin thrives.
In fact, the books this year are more resplendent
Than any season's—till the next arrives.
And poetry? Fogbound so many years,
That seacoast in Bohemia slowly clears.

Fiction, the foster child of several Muses,
Recovers somewhat from its recent binge,
Less often flaunts in print what speech refuses,
And turns to history with a tragic tinge.
Romance moves in where naturalism loses,
And Gothic doors swing out on creaking hinge.
There's much to stimulate and to beguile,
And some that's stylish at the expense of Style.

The day moves on. The sun, just past the mark
Of winter solstice, gilds an early west.
Excitement, too, fades to an afterspark;
The children murmur, and their elders rest.
The tree, however, as the hush and dark
Gather in depth, shines at its loveliest.
Now everybody, each in his way, withdraws
Into a meditative peace, because

Last night the full moon paled before a star
That blazed a path across the world beneath;
And Gaspar, Melchior, and Balthasar,
Who followed it, transmuted lore to faith;
While shepherds' pastorals were echoed far
Beyond the desert, beyond dark and death
To where—as we have read in books—was heard
The infant cry of the Incarnate Word.

Crèche

Light grow longer, dark grow less,
Heart be strong in great gladness.
Shineth Tree and pierceth Star
Where the three archangels are;
You shall know them by their wings,
And, below them, three wise kings,
And afar, where endeth night,
The incarnate Child of Light;
Maiden holy, she attendeth;
Shepherd lowly, he befriendeth;
Oxen, sheep upon their knees
Guard the sleeping Prince of Peace.
Where the Gift is given again
We uplift our hearts. Amen.

The Ruined Castle of Manorbier

It is green with ivy
But the stones are crisscrossed
With cracks and crannies,
Tooth marks of the frost.
The roofless tower,
The sundered wall,
The gaping lancet—
Frost gnaws them all.
Time in transit
Measured by years
Has emptied the hall,
Rusted the spears.
The long rains fall
Where the marriage bed
Saw the virgin a wife
And the mother dead,
Saw the birth of the son
And the warrior head
White on the pillow
Stained with red.

Now it is summer,
The swans float
Each with its double
On the scummy moat.

If you hear the fiddler
Playing his fiddle
It's the wind in the crannies
With dust in its throat.
If you hear the drummer
Tapping his drum
It's a dead branch hanging
Swinging and banging,
Summoning no one—
There is no one to come.

I was born in a chamber
Under the eaves;
The room I remember
And the sound of leaves
And the sound of ocean
And of ships come home
When we ran with our welcome
Kneedeep through the foam.

With toy sword brandished
And toy horn blowing,
Child cries to the father,
"The old raven is dead!"
And the father to the child:
"Your mother is dead!"

88

And somebody said,
"He speaks of the raven
When his mother is dead."

In the garden by moonlight
Each leaf on the rose bush
A silver flake,
A ghost of a flame!
Hearing voices, the loveless one
Fired by their passion
Fled down to the lake
Where a tall lady came.

"Tomorrow at sunset,"
She said to her lover,
"Look up to my window
And I will be there."
She glimmered away,
And faint like a halo
The moon on her hair.

Most beautiful lady,
How slowly the snail
Through the gray dust lengthens
His rainbow trail.
On the steps of the sunset

Did I find you—or not?
How should you remember
When your lover forgot?

Is there nobody now
Who can speak with my speech
But the wind in the ruin,
The waves on the beach?
There are hundreds of cities
Out there beyond reach,
Three thousand miles over
The sea whence I came.
I built them myself;
I left this to the weather,
And forgot my own name.

I will go up the stairway
That ends in the air,
I will stand in the chapel
And offer a prayer
To saints who for ages
Have not been there.
I will lean out of windows
That have no top
And look far below me
A dizzy drop

To the moat and the cliff
And beyond to the beach
And beyond to the ocean,
Where the eyes stop.

Why did I leave
   this house like a Viking?
Why did I leave it
   for frosts to crack?
Did the stairway lead me
   then to disaster?
Did the door ajar
   show the flame and the rack?
I have forgotten the cause of my going—
And even the cause of my coming back.

Some things with me
   are the never-dying,
All of us cursëd
   with time's effacement:
The ivy vine grown
   so black has forgotten
The beginning tendril
   that clung to the basement;
The gap in the wall has forgotten the window—
And I, the face that looked down from the casement.

Now is the season when the whole world over
The herds are munching the ripe clover;
The green baby-hair of the crops to come
Is ruffled by the wind; the may-flies hum
In the air, and the bees intermittently humming
Dive to one flower and drone to a sweeter:
This is the mating-song season, at evening
When the lover listens his love will be coming.

But summer like winter
Conspiring slowly
To throw down the mighty
And exalt the lowly
Is gnawing at walls
All but time held holy.
By tendrils of ivy
The stones are split;
Trees shoulder the ingles
Where earls would sit,
And the ants drag the mortar
Away, bit by bit.

Who is my brother?
Who is my friend?
The song does not falter
Though the singer end.

But I, the last singer,
Forgetting my song
One summer morning
A thousand years long,
Have gone up the stairway
That ends in the air,
Surprising dead saints
With the ghost of a prayer,
And looked out of windows
That have no top,
To the beach, to the ocean,
Where the eyes stop.
But the mind will not stop.
The heart will not stop.

ROBERT SILLIMAN HILLYER

was born in East Orange, New Jersey, on June 3, 1895. He was educated at Kent School in Connecticut, Harvard College, and the University of Copenhagen. At Harvard he won the Garrison Prize for poetry and was an editor of the *Harvard Monthly* and *Harvard Advocate*. He was a professor at Harvard for nineteen years (some of them as Boylston Professor of Rhetoric and Oratory), and has also taught at Trinity College, Kenyon College, and the University of Delaware. He won the Pulitzer Prize for poetry in 1934. In 1954 he was awarded the honorary degree of Litt. D. by the University of Delaware. Mr. Hillyer, who is a Fellow of the American Academy of Arts and Sciences in Boston and a member of the National Institute of Arts and Letters in New York, lives in Newark, Delaware.

Two type faces have been used for the composition of this book. Perpetua, designed by Eric Gill in 1927, is used on the title page, for the poem titles, and for other display lines. Bembo, a Monotype revival of one of the earliest roman types, is used for the setting of the poems. The title-page wood engraving is by Leonard Baskin. *The Relic* was composed and printed by The Stinehour Press, Lunenburg, Vermont. The paper was made by S. D. Warren Co., Boston. The binding was done by H. Wolff, New York. The typography and binding were designed by Roderick D. Stinehour.